LOOK ALIVE

Luiza Flynn-Goodlett

LOOK ALIVE

Luiza Flynn-Goodlett

SOUTHEAST MISSOURI STATE UNIVERSITY PRESS
2020

Look Alive By Luiza Flynn-Goodlett

Copyright 2020 Luiza Flynn-Goodlett

ISBN: 978-1-7320399-8-8
Softcover: $15.00

First published in 2020 by
Southeast Missouri State University Press
One University Plaza, MS 2650
Cape Girardeau, MO 63701
www.semopress.com

Cover Art: Winnie Truong
Cover Design: Diana Lieu

Library of Congress Cataloging-in-Publication Data

Names: Flynn-Goodlett, Luiza, author.
Title: Look Alive / Luiza Flynn-Goodlett.
Description: Cape Girardeau, MO : Southeast Missouri State University
    Press, 2020.
Identifiers: LCCN 2019056536 | ISBN 9781732039988 (trade paperback)
Subjects: LCGFT: Poetry.
Classification: LCC PS3606.L9388 L66 2020 | DDC 811/.6--dc23
LC record available at https://lccn.loc.gov/2019056536

For Sophia, you get it done.

CONTENTS

THE SUBLIME BEFORE (IS SOMEONE'S AFTER)

Red-throated hummingbirds spar above

the magnolia. Upwind, something grilled.

The dogs are still alive, yap at whitetail in

the cornfield. The rooster hasn't chased us

down the driveway, so no one got fed up,

loaded the shotgun. Father's heart doesn't

yet float on a pillow of fat. The miscarriage

is years off. Summers, we bleach hair with

lemon, are warm as gold on skin, haven't

glimpsed the shapes we'll be hammered in.

THINGS I COULD TELL YOU ABOUT ONIONS

I came out teeth first, took an apron string
in my mouth, stirred what was caramelizing
so she could tend to dough breathing under

a towel. Some world is always vanishing—
broth cooks off, sugar feeds yeast—still,
I strive to affix—dent others like copper,

swallow the wedding ring to keep it—most
often fail. My fire's fed with papery skins,
wrings tears, casts an uneven, amber light.

BEFORE THE BODY

We weren't yet homely—no one had noted

if baby fat melted off or took up residence,

whether we'd grown into our noses. Calves,

regardless of shapeliness, propelled us into

chlorinated depths. Only later did skin begin

to cling like a damp suit we had to claw off.

Then, we learned to favor the deck chair

rotisserie—book artfully open, slats slicing

into our backs. And forgot the deep end—

how we'd hold our breath and float above

the drain, gaze up at the distorted world.

TELL

In the end, his daughter stepped
forward, nestled the apple in her

braids, just as Joan steadied a glass,
stared down the barrel of Burroughs'
gun. Women always handle snakes

(not at the revival, but after); heart
rates lowered, adders twist wrists.

That's how mother seared the flesh
off her forearm, didn't notice until
the roast was repositioned, why we

just make sure that uncle isn't alone
with the little ones. Of course, we

take up arms—carve into cellulite,
inject wrinkles with poison—climb
atop pyres like that other, saintly

Joan. As coal, we'll scratch down
what we'd always meant to say.

AGAINST FORGIVENESS

You're told it's honey, sweet
on the tongue, a poultice for
what in you hasn't stopped

screaming. Perhaps. Others
lived through what you did,
stand upright. He has likely

forgotten too, conflated you
with another pair of ruined
tights, muddy saddle shoes.

Then why insist on calling
down this well that flings
your voice back, distorted

and faint? It's just that here,
treading water, is the child
you were, skin he unzipped

you from. Sole visitor, you
can't leave her where she was
flung ages ago. She may find

handholds in moss, climb
skyward, or drown gagging,
but you must sit, witness it.

RAGE

Steam slips between lips as I suck its wad

in my cheek, then taste iron, bit tongue.

It won't be tamed and flown, hawk-like

shadow scattering mice, yet I'm fond of

where it first entered—the centipede scar,

staple-marks scurrying up my left eyebrow.

Children reach to stroke it. Soon, all these

hairballs will be coughed up, fuse as a wick,

awaiting only a spark, whatever strikes next.

SPRING IN LARAMIE

Yawning for coffee, the exit's taken

before we mark its name. There are

bagels, cold disks of cream cheese,

then the detour snakes us away from

the highway. No brambles to stumble

or humidity to slick skin, but we know

it here, have only just begun to shed

its silences—loops of barbed wire,

and beyond, all yellow and purple,

the prairie, abloom with bruises

both faded and freshly made.

TO PENCE

It works just as you imagine,
involves as much buffoonery,

gymnastics, pauses to readjust,
switch hands. You're right, we
have at least one pair of cuffs,

varieties of lube, and get lonely,
can be found against bathroom

walls between ringlets of graffiti.
We too feared being alone with
a woman, once found her hair tie

on the rug, blond caught in metal,
saved it. We've stood at S/M-club

snack tables, tugging Twizzlers
with our teeth, yet can't count
the times we felt a body open to

pleasure, those noises it makes
like nothing you've ever heard.

LAST MOURNERS

The hearse long since
swallowed the coffin's

buffed length. Still, we
mill by the punch bowl,

veils fluttering. Such
malingering's macabre,

but we've always had
one foot in the grave—

a miscalculation, wink
in the wrong direction

from tumbling in. Then
our countrymen joined

us, albeit briefly. Quiche
munched, they've filed

into sunlight, murmuring
of all the aisles to reach

across. Soon, we'll slip
out the back, return to

accustomed places under
the steeple's sharp shadow.

FACTS OF LIFE

Death seems the most salient,
a Vantablack that flattens this
lush riot into two dimensions,

spaghettifies approaching days,
maroons us in the anxious now.
And, worse, we can't know how

tightly our watch was wound,
at what moment its whiskers
will no longer tickle, whole

mechanism stutter to a stop,
only that it must. How could
some be accorded one breath,

others a century of inhalations?
It's certainly not merit-based,
as any skinflint shivering his

dotage away can attest; eldest,
taken by fever, and youngest
(a *fag*), he's not speaking to.

Still, a certain quality of light
sneaks in sometimes, strokes
his jaw with bright fingers.

THINK WELL OF US

Though we rats fled this ship
before it sank, what little time
we had we spent gnawing rinds,

squealing. And, yes, we saw
it coming, closets of unworn
winter clothes, a bonanza for

moths. Even so, woke at noon,
ate oranges by the bagful. Can
you forgive failures, operatic

at this distance—Salton Sea
gone desert, fire ants lacing
floodwater with red ribbon.

Heat-buckled concrete tripped
us, but we caught ourselves,
kissed the top of your head in

the carrier. I know, we can't
leave you here. But we will.

TENDERIZERS

Some crack ribcages to
lift the lace of fat, weave
arteries, bypass blocks.
Third time's the charm,

he jokes, chest a mess
of staples. It's the family
affliction—what's supple
calcifies, and soon, can't

wake us. At least, that's
how grandpa went, how
we tell it. The truth is, he
courted it—drew whiskey

baths, wreathed in smoke.
And I do much the same—
array clots to spasm, cold
paddles to shock me back.

GREENBOTTLE

Princeling's gilt button, nearly knuckle-sized, you

dodge the swatter, alight just out of reach. You're

forensics' friend, first to colonize the corpse, yet,

given a living host, turn nurse, polish off diseased

tissue. What in us festered, turned rancid? Gold

filling in ash, you keep mum, gleam of the grave.

We'll mistake the flutter for blood's thrum, when

the ferryman docks, fumble you into his palm.

TO SHAMAN

After a stumbled leap from sill
to lap, you arch spine's abacus
against palm and a single purr
crests the cove of your mouth.

Shaky as a foal, you're being
born backward, not troubled
by what tugs your collar, sets
bell tinkling, instead, nose for

the fancy food we start buying.
Hours licking smoke-gray hair
into place, ambushed by sleep
in a sunbeam, belly still soft

as when you were a kitten—all
tossed like sweets from a float.
As children in the crowd, our
faces, upturned and blessed.

AT MILL CREEK

The ribcage crests ferns, slips
down the bank, is polished by

spawning salmon, unbuckled
in the stream's grasp, vertebra

masked by pine needles, mud.
Brick to body's cathedral, they

don't hint at what vigor tugged
tendons into motion, but prick—

the spindle in a fairytale. By fall,
the tabby's hit by a mail truck,

grandfather enters the hospital
with a pesky cough. Evermore

rot-filled fissures gouge world's
limestone. But, for now, white

catches light like a needle's tip,
minnows clean unseen bones.

REMAINS

Why not kneel, as sisters did,
before the pulpit and oven?
I interrogate grandma, who's

lost you amid worries that
her funeral outfit won't be
warm enough. And it's too

late to exhume buttons, root-
looped wedding ring, bones,
pitted where muscles once

held. Elsewhere, there's your
long-grown daughter, slight
Jersey accent on my tongue.

In the asylum's graveyard—
metal crosses stamped with
numbers, legend lost to fire.

But maybe it's for the best—
every indentation, a hope.

SHIPWRECK

In a crab's claw, the old door that served

as a tree house. Beneath abalone, the day

pills were pressed into your palm, mother

a month dead. You stopped crying then,

mopped the kitchen. Tides lap the milk-

glass cake stand with a final freezer-burnt

slice, saved all these years. Say, who'll take

mud-crusted labs, tell of the cobwebs slung

down banisters, how you sent us to pillage

backyard blackberries? Flights are booked,

nights driven through as surgeons scrub in

to watch your last hours molder—oranges

in a wooden bowl. At last, the ocean draws

all things to her cavernous heart. But we'll

remain, without lantern to lift to tomorrow's

dark window, see what flutters at the pane.

THE WORST

I've spent a lifetime bent to its whisper—
buckling seatbelts, checking deadbolts—
a temple scribe made to minister among

heretics streaking by on motorcycles,
scarves trailing. But, at night, converts
come—the pregnant, the pilots, those

whose fathers are newly forgetful—
array on rugs to fill lamps with fear,
which burns hotter than oil, brighter

than the match hope keeps striking,
even though the shadows capering on
my walls are lies, hardly ever arrive.

I SURVIVED

Never pick up hitchhikers, help
a man on crutches load his van.

Heed gut feelings, or else, mimic
intimacy, shield your skull, play

dead after the second shot. Take
deep breaths before being forced

underwater. Hands hacked off to
delay ID, scale the embankment,

flag a passing car. Tell everyone,
just loved ones, or no one since

you hydroplaned over it, don't
recall a thing, or do, but only

his fly popping undone, sky
searing blue beyond the trees,

the taste of rope. No one wants
to hear how time's gooey; even

now, if someone comes up from
behind, walks a certain way, you

fall back, can barely be reached—
faces haloed, streetlights in fog—

and, all the time, carry *survival*,
necessary and half-forgotten as

tampons at the bottom of a purse,
saying you've bled, still bleed, live.

I HATE A POEM WITH *POEM* IN IT

It's a southern tic—we only tell truth
to a screen door, swinging closed; never
simply ask, instead say, *Would you care*

for potatoes? wait for someone to return
the favor; despite shearling and Doc
Martens, I was sure nobody knew I'd

been playing scales along the neighbor
girl's thighs; mother only told us after
surgery, once it went well; even when

they heard I wasn't the first child he'd
pulled into those woods, no one was
called—we dissemblers, muddled as

the mint in a julep, erect monuments
to history we can't face, won't just say,
Yep, it's a poem, *now, pass the potatoes.*

HISTORY

While you never requested
passage, your passport was
stamped, forceps delivered

you into its environs. Shock
set lungs howling. Its current
tugs, but is rarely noted—father

parts a cloud of DDT, runs
after it; mother exits the dank
brownstone with an abortion;

South hocks, spits you across
the continent. It's only clear
from afar—*this* play ends in

a dead president, the blitz
begins with *that* siren. Still,
white faces squinted up at

lynched men, among them,
children still alive. And we
neglect to ask what they saw,

when they turned away, as if
today is a raft floated on, not
the wave, dragging us under.

WEEP

Seems they've seen enough, won't

stop weeping—eyes gummed, lids

fused upon waking—like two open

wounds, gashes in the meat of my

face. Can't begrudge it, only wish

they'd rolled back into the skull

to examine that fickle machinery.

But, maybe it's as intended—day,

a painterly streak, narrowed to one

foot after another, each inscrutable

face, a tulip bowed to the wind.

BIGOT SEASON

I refuse to haunt, smuggled

like lust's magma in a Victorian

letter (envelope tongued longer

than necessary). Legible as ink

down a forearm, I'm cast from

blessedly dark parking lots, pool

tables that beg to be bent over,

cigarettes ashed in every empty

vessel. No longer able to follow

a cobblestone of graves across

the Mason Dixon and be snared

in the nets of light spilling out

screen doors. But I know this

potbellied swath of states better

than it knows itself—we both

cram what alarms, along with

our longing for it, deep as a fist.

Press ears to dirt—we'll swarm,

fields husk-heavy in our wake.

WORD PLAY

We gum Lincoln Logs, drool on bibs,
but syllables, spooned with mashed

bananas, spark neurons. The moon's
bidden goodnight, Wendy takes flight.

Now, paragraph jockeys, keyboard
clackers ready with a quip, we hardly

recall the terror of cursive, when we
didn't intuit what thread binds cyanide

to an evening sky. So, how to conjure
the world before it was named? We'll

come closest bumping headboards.
As throats shudder alongside thighs,

there's no urge to transmute the golden
honey to word's bile. It's what we grope

back to—when cradled by sensation, not
yet compelled to account for ourselves.

MIRACLE FISH

Only five-and-dime purchase possible
with change from our Buick's backseat,
I shook you free and you floated, candy-

red, into my palm. Wafer of wisdom,
you were supposed to move in response
to my inquiries, but baffled with words

(*jealousy, indifference, fickle*) I'd never
encountered. Love's flash of both head
and tail was most elusive. A full-body

curl was all you'd offer. A fair mimic at
least, I held that pose for years until, fins
tongued warm, I began, at last, to dance.

PRAYER FOR APPETITE

What whispers *suckle*, tugs
spines upright, name *god*.

Acolytes—mice sniffing
a wet breeze, blouse milk-

soaked at an infant's cry,
universe ever expanding.

Oh cosmic through line,
teach the weaker sex your

bruising grip. May we find
statements heavy as stones

in throats, stay hands that
push away plates, backs

arched only to provoke
a conclusion. Instead, let

what's clenched uncoil,
pulse under the tongue.

At dawn, we'll rise to tuck
ribs into the smoker's belly.

BEFORE BABEL

As water over rocks, infant's wail, we rang
with clarity, our gratitude for being created

still a sweet, formless taffy. Leave it to Him
to take it wrong. He wanted us as flowers

seeking sun, knees sore from stone. But we
neared Him with every moan, and so, made

an offering of what in us was most alive—its
thrust direct, reaching to touch. The rest is

known. Each cursed with her own, singular
language, we roam the wilds of confusion.

THREE CHOICES

First, left she who sowed
fields with salt. Crammed

clothes in trash bags, bolted.
Second, this sea-glass coast,

moss on redwoods. Lastly,
a different woman—books

unpacked onto my shelves.
These three sketch Polaris,

point due north. But when
feverish, babbling into her

neck, it's clear that I moved
my pieces without glancing

at the board—ran to check
the mail as a plane crashed,

roof ablaze. I wasn't spared.
Didn't learn a thing. Will

stumble through the next
doorway, grope for a light.

DIORAMA

Lathed under magnifying lenses,
set with silverware, goblets that

couldn't contain a raindrop, it's
only missing the Tom Thumbs

who ducked out of sight as we
approached. Waistcoat buttons

gleaming, they'd toast whatever
Houdini shrunk, nestled them

down a dim museum corridor,
between the Japanese teahouse

and Versailles. No need to salt
venison for winter when you're

suspended in summer's comeliest
aspect, before fire razed the barn

and their only son slipped into
the river, so says the plaque. All

very accurate, historical. Perhaps
we too could claim this heaven,

preserve mattress's sag, mismatched
living room, bodies not yet run to

ruin—wailing world small enough
to be swaddled, soothed in our arms.

RELATIONAL AGGRESSION

Secretly, the bone wants to break,
and, in so doing, open a trapdoor
of skin. As bunk-bed fumblings

presaged heads bent to the lap's
salt lick, bruises are its attempts,

and *wholeness* a sleight, another
set of golden gates never opened
to you—the swelling might fade,

but teeth start to ache. So accept
weak growth plates and lug your

assigned form toward the future—
battered as an agate in the heart
of a rock tumbler, better for it.

NOTES TOWARD SOFTNESS

First, dismount the mattress.

Your grip slackens until one

finger clings. Upon release,

pray the skull's cardamom

pod crushes to fine powder,

sweet marrow drains from

limbs. Once a sieve, be run

through by woe. Darn what

baffles. What chafes, lift

to light. As necessary, cup

a loved chin or chew pastry.

Don't let blowflies alight—

their buzz of angel-flanked

gates, sealed caskets is only

noise. When tongues loosen,

stand motionless as the doe

of words noses its clearing.

Know when to dissolve,

like a salt lick, to tears.

FAMILY FRIEND

We were deft once—mended mourning
shoes with siblings' hair, closed snippets
of the hangman's rope in lockets—now

reach adulthood unscathed, spared even
a polio limp. So, how to keep you fixed
in sight? I've taken to storing bracelets

in the milk-glass cake box, painted-on
blooms like those trellising the mezcal
bottle at my wedding (a farewell party,

though we didn't know it). See, I only
eye the veil as it ripples; when it settles,
cleave back to living, hungrily. Forgive

the inattention that sweeps your visage
like leaves off a gravestone. And bless
what floats in the last smoky gulp that

I can't make myself drink. I swear, it's
a glowworm, the lunar emissary from
whatever darkness now surrounds you.

WILL

FOR MY MOTHER

She demands a burlap sack and hand-dug
backyard hole, despite questionable legality

within city limits or merits of me muscling
her in, rigor mortis and all. I ought to just

acquiesce, pump iron in preparation. But
it's the literal carrying of her death, which

I must do anyway from then on. So I offer
Arizona desert where they'd place her on

a platform to bake, sustain vultures. Even
the body farm, where she'd be tossed down

a well, bullet-riddled. But she insists, so
I picture handing shovels to siblings. And,

once the size seemed sufficient, I'd head
inside, lift her as Atlas, she, the world.

THE CHOICE

What's unthinkable, awkward
as stepping backward down
stairs, cruel as pushing aside

a home-cooked meal, seems
to me most human—embrace
the symmetry between womb

and casket, slip the overdue
book of the body down a dark
chute. Sunrise isn't assured to

any, so why direct your gaze to
the orchid, intricate as an ear's
innards, demand it be enough.

It may never be. You're still my
sister—vanished in hip-high
grass, silence that greets panic.

UNLUCKY PENNY

I know, I told you to flick it into the gutter
and turn on your heel, but lied, stowed it in

my purse's depths. I cup its glint, but it's too
humble to grant passage, entice a ferryman.

No, I'll need a coin that covers my eyes, large
enough to choke. Barring that, the pill stash

in the sock drawer will probably suffice. Abe
frowns in his cameo, drunk on superiority,

but I'm still stuck at a dead end, flipping this
cent piece, hoping, once, it comes down tails.

DARKLING

Bloody bowling ball, I come
out bald and bawling, won't
latch. When my pate fuzzes,
white as a geezer's, I speak—

too early, with a changeling's
charm. Kindergarten's sticky
mitts soon stain strands dun.
For decades, I flail in the fairy

ring—bleach it bone, streak it
rainbow, forget its true weight—
clapper ringing my skull's bell.
Only now, loam-black riven by

gray, do I return to it. As Silly
Putty pressed to newsprint, it
lapped a lifetime of dark, rests
the coiled crown at my brow.

FAGGOT

Love note slipped in the vents of lockers
I've been shoved inside, beer can lobbed

from speeding trucks, stand-in for name,
I've come to handle you gently, spare you

news of bruises, why I'm sure egg can't
be scrubbed off velvet. Years since you

were spat in my direction, hair grown out,
I've graduated to monosyllabic monikers,

but confess I miss the consonance, clarity
brought to any encounter. So, say I'll ever

be a flame-licked stick in your bundle,
my days blessed by such sweet smoke.

INOCULATION

Tuberculosis scarred your freckled
firmament with a moon. Its lamprey

kiss marks skin as organ, borders as
permeable, illusory. Legend reads—

hurt for my own good and others'. No
longer skinny-armed, curls in bows,

you avoid public restrooms, even
here, so there's no returning. Still,

you lug São Paulo—TB tests *positive*,
chest x-rays return clear—and, when

your Amazon empties into my salty
Atlantic, speak your native tongue.

TO MS. MELTON

What pricked most—my dyslexia,
her mooning, our interrupted peck

behind chessboards and dress-up
box? Childhood's sunflower seed

cracked in your teeth, shards spat
on pavement. I've met your fellows

since, loveseats zipped in plastic,
pristine cushions faded, a crisp-

cornered fraternity memory fills
like sails, or airbags the night she

was hit by a drunk driver. It was
instant, but you know how much

an instant can contain—the closet
door opens, floods two girls in light.

MIDDLE SCHOOL PRAYER

Give us heedless, skull-bashing
closeness, all lanyards and boy

bands, thighs clenched as teeth.

Let us maul ears as practice, tug
lips raw, then sleep anywhere,

through anything. But we can't

stem this current with lip gloss
and Judy Blume. As slipknots

loop new breasts, days dole out

fewer carrot sticks, crane necks
over porcelain. And there's no

one moment when we begin

to be shaved thin as truffles
onto waiting plates. No day

to travel back to, lay palms

against fevered foreheads, say,
Come with us if you want to live.

NIGHT TERRORS

The cat in my crib, I sit

on my own chest, drink

breath from my mouth,

then rise as a bat, sheets

flapping, unseeing eyes

fixed on the mute, half-

dead future, wake only

when at the front door,

jiggling its drawn bolt.

MEMORY LOSS

Siblings testify to swaddling blanket

texture as I struggle to name cousins,

huge swaths redacted by the hand that

shoved a small head toward his zipper.

It unravels—shoes wet from the stream,

lost hair ribbon, child under her desk

thinking of geodes, how she hammered

until their jeweled insides showed—into

the tangle from which I tug this thread,

too frayed to pass through my empty eye.

HOW TO TELL

When put plainly, its obscene,

artless gestures—drunk sisters

in a hammer fight—reduce us

to baser matter, body against

body, sully those who handle

it, although we never sought

it, even while it's happening,

can hardly believe it, though,

being girls, we'd prepared since

birth, and so say, *Take anything*

you want. We'll never know what

he wanted, other than a clump

of hair. You back away. Heard

enough? So, how to tell without

handing over this wet weight

like an empty overcoat? Then,

46

as you finger buttons, rummage

through pockets, explain, this is

nothing. We haven't even begun.

HE SAYS/SHE SAYS

But, she doesn't, until
he drowns in a hospital,
begging seven children's

forgiveness. Where are
the fists that sparked, set
them burning? Tongues

of flame that licked down
her throat? Underground.
His Centralia smolders—

exhales noxious vapor,
opens sinkholes to itself.
Decades later, plucking

cinders from her hair, she
remembers the night he
stopped. Mother tucked

her in instead, said, *You're
a big girl now.* And, for
better or worse, she was.

ON WANTING TO LIVE

The unfinished—teetering books

at bedside, cat mewing as her can

opens—is both burden and ballast.

Knife to oyster, it pries. The toddler

who palms a stove's red eye, fingers

sticking; doe who darts out before

a truck; jumper clawing air beneath

the Golden Gate—you're a glutton

for everything, even punishment.

SEVEN YEARS AFTER

I know, you believe in
nothing, so when you

step off the fire escape,
fall into nothing, never

bloody the courtyard's
snowdrifts. Nobody

screams, rushes down
to slick dress red. But,

as of today, I'm the older
one and can't say there's

much to recommend it,
just more living, which

you'd already tried. Yet,
you were wrong, aren't

nothing—the atoms you
animated reapportioned

to whitecaps, peaches,
ice sweating in whiskey—

an escape was impossible
from the start. It all keeps

going, takes you along for
the ride. With us. Always.

BORROWED TIME

Since unlatched baby gate tumbled
me down two stories, from loft to tile,
mother sure I hadn't survived. Since

father heard her from the creek where
he was caning chairs, and ran. Since
cracked skull, body cast. Since, nine

months old, I remember none of this.
Since dark wings swept overhead, then
retreated, father says my fontanel's web

of fractures let light in. But I know—
when the other world spread arms to
embrace, I chose this, opened my eyes.

DISCHARGE QUESTIONNAIRE

FOR MY SISTER

Though the heart thuds with *lack,*

lack, lack, do you spot its clasped

flowering—a fig's lure to wasps?

Can you conjure the tang of pencil

shavings or honeysuckle tongued

off the vine? Which path leads to

the sole's migratory eye? Yes, what

seems dawn is fire in the canyons,

but the world clasps contradictions,

doesn't deem them so. Endangered

one, let's shuck shoes, cross fields

quaking with cicadas' tredecennial

lovemaking. All creatures crave

continuation, so steady on. If we

move at a crawl, I won't mind.

A FEVER OF

This isn't some small, curated aquarium
scene, but a visitation from depths more
remote than the moon. Leaning over
the railing, we absorb their benediction—
elephant-ear wings lift wrinkles, stingers
arrest death's dominoes, as when blacking
out on BART, a voice pled, *Stay with me.*
Next time we will, for the rays that have
come, and all that will arrive hereafter.

SOFT TEACHERS

In a season of snares and hounds,
hares are nothing more than dun

flashes in foliage. Hunters hunger
as the four-footed tend burrows

of blind babies. These prophets
are as you were once—nuzzling,

barely formed. Let leaves crunch
above, dogs bark without a shiver.

Stay prey—fur glossy, eyes bright—
even when taken between teeth.

(THE SUBLIME BEFORE) IS SOMEONE'S AFTER

Both fathers grabbed them by the throat.

One uncle, drunk, drove off a bridge. Her

mother, pregnant nine times, had seven

children; his was an icicle chain-smoking

on the porch. Her pelvis, crushed under

a semi, tilted the cervical cap, so the first

of us was a *happy accident*. How remarkable

then, the veil—Queen Anne's lace, deer-cut

paths in the woods, periwinkles adorning

creek beds—drawn over all that. We wear

it still, stir delicate stitches with breath.

ACKNOWLEDGEMENTS

Acknowledgement is made to the following chapbook presses and literary publications for permission to reprint poems that appear in this book: dancing girl press, Nomadic Press; *Booth*, *Broadsided Press*, *Colorado Review*, *cream city review*, *DIAGRAM*, *Indiana Review*, *Naugatuck River Review*, *North American Review*, *The Pinch*, *Pøst-*, *Puerto del Sol*, *Quarterly West*, *Redivider*, *RHINO*, *The Rumpus*, *Salamander*, *South Dakota Review*, *Sugar House Review*, *Superstition Review*, *Tar River Poetry*, *Third Coast*

Harm's Way, dancing girl press (2019): Borrowed Time, Remains, Spring in Laramie, Last Mourners, Rage, *Faggot*, Relational Aggression, To Shaman, Shipwreck, The Choice, Weep, Night Terrors, Inoculation

Twice Shy, Nomadic Press (2020): Tenderizers, Before Babel, Unlucky Penny, Facts of Life, The Worst, Miracle Fish, Darkling, Memory Loss, On Wanting to Live, Soft Teachers

Booth: I Hate a Poem with *Poem* in It
Broadsided Press: Think Well of Us
Colorado Review: Prayer for Appetite
cream city review: Notes Toward Softness
DIAGRAM: Things I Could Tell You About Onions, Discharge
    Questionnaire
Indiana Review: Middle School Prayer
Naugatuck River Review: To Ms. Melton
North American Review: A Fever Of
The Pinch: Diorama, Three Choices
Pøst-: Word Play
Puerto del Sol: (The Sublime Before) Is Someone's After
Quarterly West: The Sublime Before (Is Someone's After)
Redivider: Bigot Season
RHINO: Greenbottle
The Rumpus: Against Forgiveness, How To Tell
Salamander: Seven Years After
South Dakota Review: To Pence, He Says/She Says, *I Survived*
Sugar House Review: Tell, At Mill Creek
Superstition Review: Before the Body
Tar River Poetry: Will
Third Coast: History

THANK YOUS

I'm immensely grateful to everyone who has enveloped me in love and support over the decade it took to write what became this, my first book—parents who dreamed this dream alongside me since I was a middle-schooler photocopying sheaves of poems at Kinkos; friends who celebrated my joy, commiserated with my despair, and attended countless weird, wonderful readings; fellow poets who modeled persistence, integrity, and community. I'm especially thankful for writing partner Sophia Starmack, and first reader Ana Anderson. And I'm deeply indebted to the vital queer force that is Foglifter Press—the editors I'm lucky enough to work alongside and the writers who trust us with their words—which taught me another, queerer world is possible, and made me feel brave enough to write toward it.

Luiza Flynn-Goodlett is the author of six chapbooks, most recently *Tender Age*, winner of the 2019 Headmistress Press Charlotte Mew chapbook contest, and *Shadow Box*, winner of the 2019 Madhouse Press Editor's Prize. Her poetry has recently appeared in *Third Coast*, *Pleiades*, and *The Common*. She serves as editor-in-chief of Foglifter and lives in sunny Oakland, California.